Contents

KV-192-087

Relatively Unscathed

IDRIS CAFFREY

Cinnamon Press

Books that are the spice of life

Published by Cinnamon Press
Meirion House
Glan yr afon
Tanygrisiau
Blaenau Ffestiniog
Gwynedd LL41 3SU
www.cinnamonpress.com

The right of Idris Caffrey to be identified as author of this work has been asserted by him in accordance with the Copyright, Designs and Patent Act, 1988.
© 2007 Idris Caffrey.
ISBN 978-1-905614-30-1
British Library Cataloguing in Publication Data. A CIP record for this book can be obtained from the British Library.

Designed and typeset in Palatino by Cinnamon Press
Cover design by Mike Fortune-Wood

Acknowledgements

Some of these poems have appeared previously in *Acorn, Aireings, The Black Rose, Borderlines, Chillout, Coffee House Poetry, Connections, Current Accounts, Decanto, The Frogmore Papers, Inclement, The Journal, Lookout, Linkway, The New Cauldron, The New Writer, Never Bury Poetry, Obsessed with Pipework, The Poetry Church, Poems in the Waiting Room, Poetry Monthly, Poetic License, The People's Poetry, Roundyhouse, Rubies in the Dark, The Seventh Quarry, The Shop, Smith's Knoll, Target, The Third Half* and *Understanding.*

Idris Caffrey was born in the market town of Rhayader in Mid-Wales. He now lives in Tamworth, Staffordshire. *Relatively Unscathed* is his sixth collection.

*For John Waddington-Feather
and Martin Holroyd*

Relatively Unscathed

Breakfast

Seven o* clock
and I start to weigh the day –
focus in on the deadlines,
measure a distance
between beginning and end.

Outside two blackbirds
suck worms from the lawn
and I stop to watch them.

They too are foraging
for a little comfort in their lives;
and me, gathering what I can
from these small pauses
between light and dark.

Lines

Weeds and long grass
now cover the railway line –
there is no longer that crunch
of stone underneath my feet
like soldiers marching off to war.
The signals are down,
the embankment crumbles away,
the seasons run their course.

I know that if I return again
or never return, the signs of man
will soon be swept away,
only memories will stay,

I will be that old man
in the pub who remembers –
who tells the story of the railway line
to half-listening youths, who stare
into the darkness of their mobile phones.

After the Party

The house is pale
with shock, flinches beneath
the rubbish strewn in every room.

Dishes pile higher
with every thump of the clock
while through thin curtains I can see
some semblance of a day best shut out.

In the petrified air
I catch a trace of your scent –
follow it through the hall, glimpse a face
in a mirror that doesn't look like me at all.

Uncomfortable Shoes

I place the shoes on the highest rock,
begin to weigh their worth:
they were never any good.

So I leave them there –
leave them to the wind and rain,
a sacrifice to the season's attrition.
I leave them for the traveller
for the journeys still to make –
I leave them for the philosopher
to ponder the mysteries of the world –
I leave them open-mouthed
for the people who cannot speak.

Bare foot and running free
I plunge through ferns to the waiting valley.

Plateau

"...in the slower
World of the poet you are just coming
To sad manhood... "
                    R.S.Thomas

You were too old,
I couldn't listen to your words
but left them to fall away
empty of meaning.
I was like one of your congregation
who came not to grow
but register their tick for Heaven.

I went my own way,
trod the poet's path
through the wanton years
then on through the darkness,
until I stood on a plateau
where I looked over and saw
a frail light beckoning on the other side.

With the Snow

All day poems have fallen
with the snow,
onto the silent earth below.
Released from the heavens
to fly free,
they take that journey of uncertainty.

Some people step inside
leave the day,
but a few will wait and
watch them play,
try to cup them in their hands
to read before they melt away.

Mushrooming

Today I will hunt for mushrooms.

I drive a hundred miles
to the place I knew so well.
Even after all this time
the field looks the same —
gate locked, curls of October mist
heaving from the grass.

I crawl through the bars,
stride out towards the clouds,
one eye for the farmer,
the other for small white angels
lifting from the wet ground.

But there are none,
not one single mushroom
anywhere to be seen
and the motionless cows
stare at me across the lost years
and I can only stare back.

Gradual Changes

Autumn has come early
and the leaves fall around me
in the heat of a summer afternoon.

Am I a witness to the World changing,
the seasons shuffling about,
lost in confusion and time somehow out?
Ah no, these things, I am told, take longer –
thousands of years, maybe more,
the earth stiffened in summer –
snow stacked high to the top of the house wall.

And a silence unknown,
which a poet could write about forever –
if he were but there.

Dunes

We stand at the top, holding hands,
bare feet tickled by matted grass.
Only the whispers of waves,
jabbing at the shore,
break the silence,
a background to our hesitancy.

Then we leap,
free-fall together,
drop like sea birds through summer,
until warm sand engulfs us
and we laugh because we're safe.

The sun sinking down
but still holding us gently into the day.

Waiting for Monday

There are words I should have said,
instead I think them, sit here and think them
but I hear my mother's voice once more –
It is never good to think too long.
So I begin to whisper to the walls,
then shout them at the sleeping
earth beneath the floors –
hurl them through the window
at the roses until their blood-red petals fall,
their sharp thorns turn away towards the street
and Monday cannot hurt me anymore.

Wales in Springtime

for Ralph Hill

There is more here
than the outward signs of spring,
those few bright primroses,
the many shades of green.
Two buzzards circle overhead:
mapping the future
from the embers of the past.
I can only stand and watch –
caught between a sense of hope
and the sense of something lost.

Tony Climbs the Tree

It took him twelve years
to finally climb that tree,
reach the first branch
and swing his leg over
to sit on the wrinkled bark.

How different the world looked –
a sky hidden by leaves,
the earth unable to touch him anymore.
He had done it at last
but it didn't seem enough,
so up, up into the highest branches
and further still until an old man
found him as white as an angel
on the ever darkening ground.

Relatively Unscathed

I drive past kale fields –
blurs of yellow gold.

I have burnt away the miles
and wandered far from those dreams
that were there at the start.
The years have come and gone
and now there is only acceptance –
a thankfulness almost that I came
through relatively unscathed.

The yellow fields are behind me,
grey rain in chasing the day
and words fall around me in whispers –
drive on, drive on, they say.

Two Sightings

You were unexpected,
coming as you did in daylight,
and for a moment, fox and man
stopped to size up those barriers
behind each other's frightened eyes.

I find you later on a slip-road,
your cunning already stripped
and as cold as the frosted dark,
as 1 lay you gently on the stiffened grass.

Some way off, I can hear your cubs
whimper softly, but the place is lost
beneath the noise of a man hammering
the dent out of the body of his car.

Amsterdam Drizzle

The streets are soaking,
puddles open their mouths
in silent screams.
Empty tram cars
rattle by
certain of the way.

And my life too
is hurrying somewhere,
I hug my coat around me,
finding no shelter from the rain.

The Other Side of the Valley

The sun has come out late today
and lights the golden fields,
making them look nearer now.
The hay is waiting to be gathered,
rolled up in neat carpets,
soaking the last warmth of pale sunlight

I would like to go to the hills,
watch the shadows from hedges
close in until there is nothing left
but one small wedge of light
that you can hold in your hand
and throw up into the darkening sky
to burst into a million tiny stars.

Light Years

It's nearly dusk but my father
takes an axe into the lower field
and starts chopping down a conifer tree.
With every shuddering blow
a gasp of snow falls from the branches –
it will be Christmas soon.

I ask if I can help
but he sends me away to my room –
he spends more time with my sister now
and I've often heard her crying.
Yesterday I came up behind her
as she was watching the frozen lake
and touched her on the arm;
she flinched as if stung by a bee
and turned around with frightened eyes
but gave a small, almost forgotten smile,
when she saw it was only me.
We walked home together,
separated by a long width of cold
and there was so much I wanted to know.

The tree in the lower field is down,
another space given back to the sky
and millions of stars are coming out of the dark.
I blow out the candle, say a small prayer,
listen for footsteps coming up the stairs.

Today

Only a frail sprinkling of snow,
not going to alter much –
brooding mountains regain their poise,
the day returns to icy blue.

This – the scene for today,
the backdrop to where we are
and what we have become.
A world always changing,
keeping its distance,
seasons never doing quite enough
until we step from behind
the glass and run out into our lives.

At Abergwesyn

I sit in the silence
where earth and sky meet –
in the pause between
this world and the next.
There is no other place
I know like this;
no other place as still,
nowhere so far away
from the life I have to lead.

I watch the brown stream
trickling its way to the sea,
a tapestry of clouds
shifting shadows all around me.
The hours pass into dark
as a bird falls like a tear
shed in the night, lit
for a second by the smouldering
remains of the light.

Famous for the Day

Nobody had much time for him,
thought him a bit odd living
up there so near the clouds.

Mysterious circumstances,
took him, all the rooms
full of poetry, they say.

All cleared away now –
dreams thrown out in bundles
wrapped with brown string.

I still go up there sometimes
to feed the pigeons
that wait on the windowsills.

Prayers

Prayers are falling everywhere,
from enormous buildings
and small quiet rooms.
I sometimes hear their chatter
in the nearby woods when I
close the window on the night –
but then leave it open for a little while
to hear the whispered platitudes.

While others return to greet the day,
these must be prayers that are pushed away,
unanswered hopes that journey back
to break the dreaded fear of dark.

Crossroads

Under the bridge leaves gather
like birds ready to go.
The river plays with them,
plunges them into the dark depths
before easing each one gently
into collages on quiet pools.

Soon they will be gone.
I will look down from the bridge
 and autumn will be just a memory,
a vague recollection that time allows
like the grey faces staring up at me
from beneath the cracking ice.

Three Journeys

Out of the safety of the warm dark
to the long road through the mist –
wheat bending in the breeze,
the rooks scattered out across
the first sprinkling of snow in the fields.
That twinning of darkness and light
at dawn just as a pale sun
crawls up from behind the trees
and autumn's leaves ignite
in the pause before they fall.

This journey we know,
always under the curious stars –
the never ending constellations
that light our way to another world.

Bubbles

Somewhere a child
is blowing bubbles —
small balls of rainbows
that fall all around me.

I too had dreams
and as the last bubble
rests in my hands,
I start to make them again.

Secure Wing

They gaze out at the world
from the other side of the glass,
for me the day is bitter cold –
for them the frost is jewels they cannot hold.
When I smile, it is a false smile
fashioned out of misunderstanding,
but theirs welcomes me into the fold.

They wave as I go outside
to my world on the other side
and I wave back, no longer feeling the cold
while night sparkles around me with new stars.

Someone Else

He tells her
this isn't him –
it's someone else,
as he wipes the blood
from her mouth.

He's been someone else
for so long now
she can't remember
who he really was.

Sometimes whispers creep
into the thumping in her head –
words about love,
something about love.

Welsh Poppies

Far from home
and all that time spent
trying to grow Welsh poppies
in your garden in England.
Meconopsis cambria, you called them
and every year you watched
for their frail flowers.

But nothing came,
only the years that slipped away
until I was left alone
looking out across the river,
where Welsh poppies glow
like stars, to smooth
the trembling shadows of the dark.

Dream Sequence

Wreaths of Michaelmas daisies,
moths beat against the walls,
a finger writes on a cold window
and autumn's poems
run away on streaming glass.
Then a silent church wedged
into the depths of winter
with a small boy among
gravestones feeding birds
as trees bend under the shock of frost
and a path of angels guide him home.
A man walking on a beach,
gulls rise in silent screams,
while the sea's music breaks and scatters,
wipes out all traces of where he's been.
The house silent, candles flicker,
damp wood hissing in the hearth
where faces stare and are gone
in twists of smoke that linger on
for centuries in the shadowy hall
and then turn to scattered stones.
The lover picking straw
from auburn hair after the sun
has melted them together
and love is whispered into a summer
they surely thought would last forever.
Poppies waving in golden fields
as they awaken in separate lives,
love so freely given, but so hard to receive.

I wake as the day spills
through curtains in a blaze of light
and dreams and pestering truths
are already trying to find their way back
into the dark pockets of the night

Sermon

My mind turned
from the voice in the pulpit
so it became distant,
like a whisper from Heaven.
I counted the rows of pews
relentless in emptying out
the generations and watched
an old man praying for
a little more time to stay.
A captured moth
beat against the windows
trying to rejoin the red autumn
where conkers crashed through leaves
and other boys picked the treasure.
The light fading, a lone candle
waiting for the stirring dark.

Snow

Stillness, sudden warmth,
a few small flakes falling
then growing like memories.

I look into the sky,
let the swirling snow take me.
Sledges, the shrieks of children
and a small room darkening
with the last embers of a fire,
until I find myself standing in the rain.

Pen-y-Garreg Dam

It's always disappointing
when the dam is not flowing over —
the black waters so still and cold,
grey stones unmoved, holding it all back,

I sit for an hour
waiting for something to happen –
but there's only the pale clouds,
drifting aimlessly to nothing,
the brown fern dying all around me.

I don't know what I expected –
maybe that very same morning,
somehow frozen in time:
white water cascading over the walls,
spray bursting into our smiling faces;
the wonder of it all, that tingle of fear
and a squeezed hand,
telling me that she was still there.

Dandelions

Dandelions unfurl from the dark,
their small suns winking in the grass.
How unwanted they always are
and we've destroyed almost
everything else by war,
but these lost souls still endure.

I will leave them grow this year,
blow the seeds far away
and make three wishes just once more.

Out There

I look over the gardens
to the far fields –
the harvest gathered,
a thousand rooks rising
from their foraging among the stubble.

I don't know what frightened them,
there is nothing that I can see
and I wait for their black wings to return
out of the red fires of the sky.
But they don't come back
and I find myself drawn away
like a sleep-walker, stepping out
over the very edges of the dark.

Place

High on the hills
the centuries pass unnoticed,
while a buzzard circles
for scraps of the dead
and the stones in the fields
cry out to be heard
as moss suffocates their screams.

Down in the valley
church bells no longer ring,
people shuffle their lives about
in the shadows of the winding streets
and do not speak, for there
are no words left to say –
only thin echoes snigger from the past.

And it is a dream,
a recurring dream I have
of a place that I once knew
but the morning sun awakens me
to all those things I hold true –
the dream lied, as dreams so often do.

Red Flowers

Just for the day
the red flowers bloom.
Planted in the wrong place,
at the wrong time by someone else,
I leave them in a state of some neglect.

So thin and frail,
pale red flowers as if the blood
had been drained from their very souls.

Every year I wait for them,
watch for the tiny red flowers
to come again, and they do.

Schoolroom

Trying to see in
through the frosted windows,
I heave myself up onto a ledge
and wipe the glass with my glove.

There is little to see –
the room is empty now
so I try to fill it again
with relics from the past –
lift-up desks. Miss Middlefield
and the chalk dust that spun
in the beams of light
tilting through the glass.

Few images come though
and I drop to earth once more –
wonder why we are drawn back
to our beginnings almost as if
we can start anew from here.

It's starting to snow –
I fear it will be a long journey home.

The Last Day of Autumn

Late in the afternoon
the sun finally cracks the mist
and falls on the beech tree,
whose leaves have not yet fallen,
so summer seems to live again.

And I go out into the garden,
through the wet grass,
to feel the warmth
and watch the sunbeams'
dance along the branches
while the birds sing again.
But it doesn't last,
the sun drops behind the hill
and the day retreats into the dark.

I walk back
through the sudden cold –
leave the seasons to run their course
and behind me the beech leaves
weep as they fall.

Tallies

Somewhere your finger is tracing
numbers on a cold window
as swallows gather ready to go –
the changing world scratches
one more day on my bones.
Another season turning around –
soon the first frosts will
harden the miles between us
and your face will be just a memory
to cheer the long dreams of winter
like a butterfly spread out in snow.

One Daffodil

You hove come too soon
I am not ready for you yet —
my mind is set in Winter,
the cold is in my head.
But you are suddenly here as if
sent from another time,
a different world of endless days
when I ran in fields of yellow flowers.

Every day I watch you –
doing what you can to stay
but you were never strong,
a lone candle trying to light the dark
and Spring engulfs you in its flames.

Elan Valley

A yellow balloon
floats down the valley,
eased by the wind
towards the town.
I watch it go,
its uncertain journey
soon fades to a memory –
rain, earth, rock,
this enduring sky
unmoved by its intrusion.
Only I am surprised,
wonder at its questions –
so brief its stay, so brief mine.

Horses in Winter

They stand patient and still,
watching the world from afar
as if not part of it anymore –
their steaming breath taken away
by the cold clutches of the day.
I always stop to watch them –
there is something that draws me
to their doleful eyes,
while across the frosted fields
they have left symbols for our luck,
horseshoes printed in the hardened mud.

I think they will stand forever
shuddering at the end of every day,
silent as graves and long betrayed;
waiting for the first bright star
to draw the dark around them –
hide the centuries of dismay.

Ten Minutes of Daylight

They say this is the place
for the best view of the city,
but I have come here late
in the lull before dark.

There are times when we know
we will not return again
so I try to take it all in –
like drawing a last breath.

Now the orange lights are on
and I know its all over,
this small impression of a world
as far away as the sudden stars.

Jumping into Rhododendrons

Late May and summer's promises
thicken with the scent of evening.
I stand on the railway embankment
looking down on the massed
rhododendrons,
wondering if I should jump.
The others are not with me now –
that summer we thought
would last forever has now long gone.

I weigh the drop, begin to lose my nerve
but have already too many regrets,
take one deep breath and launch
myself into the uncertain darkness.
I need not have worried though,
the branches cushion me, gently release me
and let me slip down again to the soft earth.

A few scratches, that's all,
and I crawl out to find the sun,
stand there a while before I walk on.

Room Eight

They tell me it's quite common
at this stage, to drift into the past,
to remember childhood vividly
when she can't even remember her name.
Perhaps that's the only time we're happy
and then forget how to be
as our lives turn to face the world.

She looks up at me, into a face
that hasn't been born yet
and smiles at who is to come.

Old Radnor

I have passed it often
up there chiselled into the hill.
Rolled carpets of hay
lie spread out at its feet,
the church bouncing light
off its windows like beacons
of hope in a darkened age.

It isn't that I haven't
had time to visit the place,
only that I prefer to leave it there
to turn with the seasons –
something beautiful like love,
often, distant but not
completely out of reach.

Poems in Cwmdonkin Park

I read once more
his words hewn into Welsh rock —
Time held me green and dying
Though I sang in my chains like the sea.

Little has changed here
in this small park on the hill –
rain still burrows through the shrubbery,
birds shake out their tired wings.

The years have rolled by
and as I stand looking out across the bay
the words of my first poem come again,
so thin and frail, but mine.

Short Walk in Winter

My usual walk
around the block –
nobody about,
the same stop
to watch the sad horses
standing in the fields.
Then it's up the hill,
down through factories
where a small gesture
of newly planted trees
are shocked to stillness
by their first covering of frost.

Soon it will be dark,
the day so quickly done –
I close the door to the night
as the pale sun again tries
leaving something for tomorrow.

Candlelight

I light a candle,
fashion the dark
into figures on the wall –
buzzards gliding over pine trees,
a fox skulking across a field.

Shadows of memories,
enduring against the city cold,
the blue sirens racing for a life
and I will hold them
until my fingers close.

Far Away Places

I sit under the shade
of an olive tree,
wash my face with
the water from a fountain.

Silver coins shine
up at me –
a hundred wishes
sparkling from the depth
of the shimmering pool.

The scorching sun
bums even deeper
into the dusty track
and there is no escape
from the journey back
to all of my mistakes.

I too make a wish,
then pick my first olive
and bite into its flesh
expecting, all the time.
that it will be sweet.

Backyard

A small tree, broken wall
and a coal shed –
that's what I would tell you
if you happened to ask me
to describe my childhood backyard.
Perhaps I would also mention
the blue swing rusting in the snow.

But if you probed a bit deeper,
I might go a bit further
and give you more than just clues.
Here were the skeletons of my being,
here the dreams I took away
for all the years ahead.

So ask the right questions
and you will find me –
the tree now gone,
that broken wall mended
and my absence buried
like the forgotten coals
deep beneath the ground.

Poetry

How did it come?
This thing called poetry –
did it find me,
or I, looking for something else,
suddenly found it
like a lost key on the stairs?
Startled by the singing of birds,
the gentle tap of snowflakes on a window,
I begin to write it all down
but find nobody else can hear.

The years pass
and I'm starting to unravel your secrets,
beginning to look, beginning to listen,
am able to hold a few words in my hands –
perhaps at last the journey can start.

We hope you have enjoyed this book from
Cinnamon Press.

Cinnamon publishes the **best in poetry, fiction and
non-fiction**.

For writers – bi-annual competitions in four genres
– first novel, novella, short story & first poetry
collection. Cash prizes and publishing contracts.

For book lovers - great poetry and fiction titles from
the best new names as well as established writers.

For the best amongst poetry journals: *Envoi* –
celebrating 50 years of poetry

For a full list of titles visit: www.cinnamonpress.com

Cinnamon Press Writing Awards:

We run four writing competitions with two deadlines each year – the genres are – Debut Novel; First Poetry Collection; Novella; Short Story

Deadlines June 30th and November 30th each year.
All entries by post + sae & details - name, address, email, working title, nom de plume.

Novel: 1st prize - £500 + publishing contract. Submit 10,000 words. 5 finalists submit full novel & receive appraisal. Entry - £20 per novel.

Poetry Collection: 1st prize - £100 & publishing contract. Runners up published in anthology. Submit 10 poems up to 40 lines. Three finalists submit further 10 poems, any length. Entry - £16. per collection, includes free copy of winners' anthology.

Novella: 1st prize - £200 + publishing contract (20 – 45,000 words). Submit 10,000 words. Four finalists submit full novella. Entry - £16 per novella.

Short Story: 1st prize - £100 & publication. 10 runners up stories' published in winners' anthology. Length 2,000 – 4,000 words. Entry - £16 per story, includes free copy of winners' anthology.

Entries to: Meirion House, Glan yr afon, Tanygrisiau, Blaenau Ffestiniog, Gwynedd, LL41 3SU

Full details www.cinnamonpress.com